God
Made Big Plans
for You

Rose Perrone

ISBN 978-1-68526-090-3 (Hardcover)
ISBN 978-1-68526-091-0 (Digital)

Covenant Books, Inc.
11661 Hwy 707
Murrells Inlet, SC 29576
www.covenantbooks.com

To the Lord. He has led my life and has given me the inspiration to write this beautiful work.

For Everett, my precious gift from above.

God has fearfully and wonderfully made you.

—Psalms 139:14

Sit awhile here with me as I rock you in my arms, as I take in all that God has fearfully and wonderfully made you to be.

Even the very hairs of your head are all numbered.

—Matthew 10:30

But this time is short because I know that God has made big plans for you someday soon.

He has humbly made you for His work.

He has tenderly made you, knowing all the hairs on your head.

He has perfectly made you just as you are.

For I know the plans I have
for you declares the Lord.
Plans to prosper you and not
to harm you. Plans to give
you hope and a future.

—Jeramiah 29:11

Sit awhile here with me as I whisper sweet prayers into your ear. Time is running away because God has made big plans for you someday soon. He has made plans to prosper you. He has made plans to give you hope. He has made plans to give you a future.

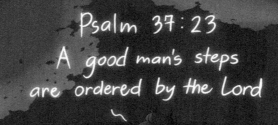

Psalm 37:23
A good man's steps
are ordered by the Lord

The steps of a good and righteous man are
directed and established by the Lord. He
delights in his way and blesses his path.

—Psalms 37:23

Sit awhile here with me as you rest your head on my shoulder. I know someday you will be grown into the man God has made you to be, because God has made big plans for you someday soon.

A man God has ordered his footsteps.

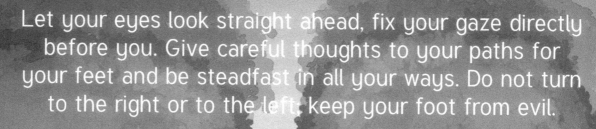

Let your eyes look straight ahead, fix your gaze directly before you. Give careful thoughts to your paths for your feet and be steadfast in all your ways. Do not turn to the right or to the left; keep your foot from evil.

—Proverbs 4:25–27

A man God has chosen.
A man God has called.

The Lord your Creator, He who formed you says,
I have called you by name and you are mine.

—Isaiah 43:1

Sit awhile here with me as I sing sweet songs with you. Tears rolling down my cheeks to a happy tune that will forever live in my heart.

I close my eyes and take it all in as this will all be just a sweet memory because I know that God has made big plans for you someday soon.

Even before He made the world, God loved us and chose us.

—Ephesians 1:4

God has prepared your life.

God has loved you every day.

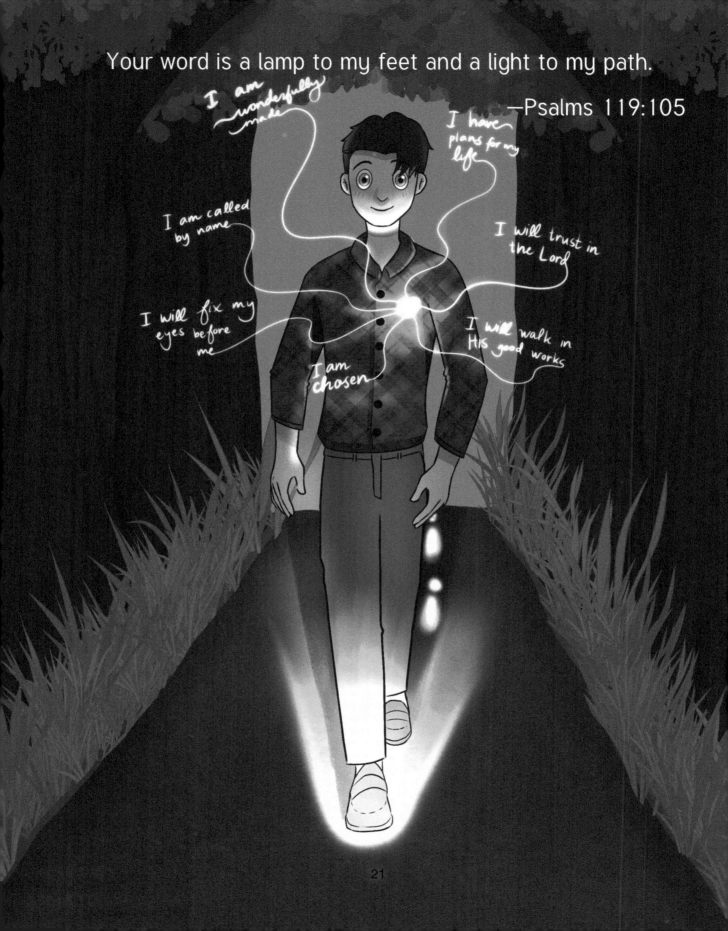

God has chosen you for His purpose.

With all prayer and petition pray with specific requests, at all times, on every occasion and in every season.

—Ephesians 6:18

Because God has made big plans for you...someday soon.

About the Author

Rose Perrone grew up in Brooklyn, New York, and currently resides in Long Island with her husband and her son, Everett. She is a nurse practitioner and teaches nursing education. This is her first publication. Every night, she rocked Everett to sleep, praying over him and for the plans God has prepared for him. She realized how fleeting this precious time with her son was and one day he would be grown. She wanted to teach him how to come into agreement with God's plans for his life. Her inspiration had come after an empty pursuit of a story that would ignite and engage Everett's imagination about his prosperous future. Rose has envisioned God's spoken word, coming to life and applied personally, just as God has intended for everyone.

CPSIA information can be obtained
at www.ICGtesting.com
Printed in the USA
JSHW062149260922
31038JS00002B/45

9 781685 260903